MY FIRST STORYBOOK

BIBLE

This book belongs to:

_____

It was given to me by:

_____

On:

_____

SCANDINAVIA

CONTENTS

THE OLD
TESTAMENT

DAY AND NIGHT BEGIN

Genesis 1–3

Before there were butterflies, trees, or water,

God created the universe and placed the sun

in the sky to light up our days.

God filled the earth with all kinds of
animals, from shy zebras to sneaky foxes,
and from colorful parrots to spotted
cheetahs. Next He created people, a man
and a woman, so they could enjoy life
with Him. God liked everything He had
made very much!

"You may eat the fruits from all the trees except one," God said. But one day, a snake tricked Adam and Eve into eating the forbidden fruit. Adam and Eve had sinned against God and could no longer live in the garden with Him.

SAVED FROM THE RAIN IN A BOAT

Genesis 6:5-8:22

Sadly, people started to forget about God and just wanted to live their lives on their own, without His love. As the years passed, the world grew cruel. This made God very, very sad.

But Noah loved God, and God loved Noah. "Noah," said God one day, "I will send a flood to wipe out evil. But I will save you and your family."

Noah had three sons: Shem, Ham, and Japheth. "God told me to build a huge boat because a heavy rain will come," Noah said. "Thanks for helping me build it!"

Finally the boat was finished! Then Noah gathered the animals. "Make sure you get two of each kind! Don't leave any out," God said.

Rain poured down for many days,
flooding the earth. As the water rose,
Noah, his family, and all the animals
were safe inside the boat.

After 40 days and 40 nights, the rain stopped, and the skies started to clear. God put a rainbow in the sky as a sign of His promise: "I will never flood the earth like this again!"

GOD KEEPS HIS PROMISES

Genesis 15; 18:1-15 & 21:1-6

Abraham and Sarah were old. "You will have a son," God told them, "and your familiy will be very big."

Now Abraham was almost one hundred years old and still they had no son. Abraham trusted that God would do what He promised.

Abraham and Sarah waited for many
years, and God kept the promise
He gave them. One day Sarah and
Abraham had a baby boy. They named
him Isaac. "God has kept His promise
by giving us Isaac," Sarah said. Isaac
was the first of many children in
Abraham and Sarah's big family.

A DREAM COMES TRUE

Genesis 37; 39–47

Joseph had ten older brothers. "In my dream, we were in a big field binding hay into bundles. My bundle was in the middle, and yours all gathered around it, bowing down to my bundle as if I was your ruler," he told his family.

"You will never rule us!" Joseph's
brothers sneered. They hated him
because of his dreams and because their
father loved Joseph more than them.
One day they sold Joseph to traders
travelling to a faraway country.

The traders went to Egypt. There Joseph
became a slave. He worked hard and always
did his best. God was with him, and soon
everyone liked him very much.

One day the king of Egypt had a dream. No one knew what it meant. Then they asked Joseph. "Your dream is a warning from God," Joseph told the king. "A famine will hit the country, so you should be prepared." The king made Joseph his helper and asked him to gather food for the famine.

The famine also struck the land where Joseph's brothers lived. They travelled all the way to Egypt to buy food. There they bowed down to Joseph, the ruler, just like he had seen in his dream! "You meant to harm me!" Joseph said. "But look: God has used this for good!" And Joseph forgave the harm his brothers had done to him.

GOD CHOOSES MOSES

Exodus 2:1-14:31

Joseph and his brothers moved to Egypt to live. They grew in number, and this made the new king of Egypt afraid. He made them his slaves and ordered all the Hebrew baby boys to be killed. Moses' mother hid him in a basket among the river reeds. There he was found by the princess. "He is so cute. I will keep him!" she giggled.

Moses grew up as an Egyptian prince.
One day Moses saw an Egyptian beating a
Hebrew. Moses got so angry that he killed
the Egyptian man. When the king found out,
Moses was in trouble. He had no choice but
to run far away from Egypt.

Moses ended up in the desert. There he became a shepherd. One day, as Moses was watching his sheep, God spoke to him from a burning bush. "Moses," said God, "go back to Egypt and tell the king to let my people go free!"

After a long time, the king of Egypt gave in. Moses led the Hebrews out of Egypt. "Look! God is splitting the sea in two so we can walk right through it. Now we are safe!" they said to each other.

GOD HAS BLESSED US

Ruth 1-4

Naomi was an old woman who lived in a foreign land. She was very sad because her husband and two sons had died. "I'm all alone now," she said. "I will go back home!" Ruth had been married to one of Naomi's sons, and she said, "I will come with you; you will not be alone."

When they came back home to Bethlehem, they didn't have much. They had little food and no one to take care of them. They were poor and alone. Don't worry!" said Ruth. "I will go look for food for us."

Ruth found a field that was being harvested. She started to gather the left-over grain. It was there that she met Boaz. He was a kind and caring man. "Take as much grain as you want," Boaz told her.

Not long after, Boaz and Ruth got married. "How God has blessed us! Now we have a family again. We have someone to care for and someone who cares for us!" said Ruth and Naomi.

WHO CALLED SAMUEL?

1 Samuel 3:1-10

Samuel was a young boy who lived in the tabernacle, the place where people worshiped God. It was late at night when Samuel heard a voice call, "Samuel, Samuel!"

"Eli," said Samuel to the old priest who slept nearby, "Did you call me?"

"No," said Eli. "Maybe it was God?"

When Samuel heard the voice calling his name again, he prayed, "Yes, God, I am listening." As Samuel grew up, he learned to recognize God's voice and became an important prophet.

THE BOY WHO FOUGHT THE GIANT

1 Samuel 17

David had seven older brothers. He was also a shepherd taking care of his father's sheep. "Have a great day, Dad!" he said before he went out to the flock.

David had to fight off a bear and a lion that tried to snatch a lamb away from him. "Dear God, please protect me!" David prayed as he chased them both away.

David's brothers were at war. "I am the strongest. None of you can beat me!" the giant enemy soldier Goliath shouted. When David brought food to his brothers, he heard Goliath's boasting.

"I will fight this giant!" David told the king. "God protected me against the bear and the lion, and He'll help me against Goliath." David went out and picked up stones for his slingshot at a nearby creek.

When Goliath saw David, he shouted, "Who do you think you are? You don't look like a warrior. You don't even have a sword!" Goliath laughed at David.

David replied, "You have a sword, but I have the living God on my side!" David ran towards Goliath and threw a stone from his sling.

The stone hit Goliath right in the forehead, and the giant fell to ground. "Thank you, God!" David thought as everyone started to celebrate.

"Yes! David won!" they shouted.

A WISE DECISION

1 Kings 3:5-10; 6

Solomon had just become king of Israel. "Ask for one thing you would like from Me," God told Solomon, "and I will give it to you!"

"I ask for the wisdom to be a good king," Solomon replied.

God was very pleased that Solomon didn't ask for lots of money and great fame. God gave Solomon wisdom and made him the wisest king ever. Men and women came from far and wide to learn from him.

"I will build a temple for God," Solomon decided. "It will be a beautiful place for people to worship God and pray to Him."

GOD IS ALIVE

1 Kings 18:16-45

Elijah loved God, but most people had forgotten about Him. Instead they worshipped false gods made of stone and wood. This made Elijah very sad. "Why are they doing what is wrong?" Elijah thought. He decided to do something to show people who was the one true God—the statues of stone and wood or his God.

Elijah told everyone to gather on a mountain and said. "Let's both make altars. You ask your false gods to light a fire on your altar, and I will pray to the living God to light a fire on mine." Nothing happened when the people prayed to their false gods.

"God, let all people know that You are the true God!" Elijah prayed. God showed Himself to be mighty by sending down fire on Elijah's altar and burning everything up—even though it was soaking wet! The people now realized that only God was living and true.

THE BOY WHO KEPT HIS FAITH

Daniel 1; 6:1-25

Many years later, a war broke out in Israel. A young man named Daniel was captured with his people and taken to a country far, far away.

The king liked Daniel because he was wiser than the other students. The king gave Daniel an important job as his helper. "I wish the king didn't like him so much," some jealous people whispered. "Let's make the king get rid of Daniel!" Daniel, meanwhile, kept his faith and always prayed to God.

The jealous people tricked the king into making a new law. The law said that anyone who prayed to someone besides the king would be thrown into the lions' den. When Daniel prayed to God, the jealous people told the king about it. The king was very sad.

"I cannot change the law," the king told Daniel, "but may the God you pray to protect you!"

Then Daniel was thrown into the den of lions, and he stayed the whole night in there. God did not forget about Daniel, and He sent an angel to shut the mouths of the lions.

The next morning, the king rushed
to check on Daniel. "Are you
alive? Has your God protected
you?" the king shouted.

"Yes, God sent an angel to watch
over me!" Daniel answered, and
the king set him free.

THE MAN WHO RAN FROM GOD

Jonah 1–3:3

"Go tell the people of Nineveh to stop being so evil!" God said one day to His friend Jonah. "Otherwise I will punish them." Jonah did not want to go to Nineveh. He didn't like the people from Nineveh at all. In fact, he hoped that God would punish them. So Jonah went on a boat far away from the city of Nineveh.

At sea, a mighty storm broke loose and huge waves were almost sinking the ship. "What is happening?" the sailors asked each other.

Jonah admitted that he had run from God and now God had sent the storm. "Throw me overboard. Then the storm will end," Jonah said.

The storm ended as Jonah sank down into the sea. "Help me, God!" Jonah prayed. God sent a huge fish that swallowed him up, and for three days Jonah was inside the fish.

"What have I done, trying to hide from you God?" Jonah prayed. "You are the one that saves. Thanks for saving me! I will give thanks to you and praise you always!"

God then told the fish to cough up Jonah.
Again, God told him go to Nineveh, and
this time Jonah went. He understood that
God wanted to give the people in Nineveh
a second chance, just like God had given
him a second chance, too.

THE NEW
TESTAMENT

WHEN JESUS WAS BORN

Luke 2:4-16; Matthew 2:9-11

Many years later, a man named Joseph and
his fiancée Mary had to travel all the way
to Bethlehem. Mary was pregnant. She was
expecting a boy—not just any boy, but God's own
son, Jesus. "Let's look for a place to stay; the
baby will arrive soon," Mary told Joseph.

A lot of other people had traveled to Bethlehem also. "All our guest rooms are already taken," the innkeeper told Joseph and Mary when they tried to find a place to sleep. "I can only offer you the barn."

"A barn will have to do," said Joseph.

That night Mary gave birth to baby Jesus and wrapped Him in cloths and laid him in the manger. Shepherds heard angels tell them about their newborn king. "He is the promised savior!" the angels said.

"We too have come to see the child who will be king of the Jews," the wise men said. They brought precious gifts of gold, incense, and myrrh.

JESUS CALLS HIS DISCIPLES

Matthew 4:19

Jesus chose twelve special friends to follow Him. He taught them about God and showed them His love! The twelve friends became Jesus' disciples.

NATURE OBEYS JESUS

Mark 4:35-41

A mighty storm surprised the disciples when they were out sailing. They were terrified, but Jesus was sound asleep in the boat. "Wake up, Jesus!" the disciples cried. "We are all going to drown!"

Jesus woke up and said, "Be still waves! Be quiet storm!" Immediately the sea was calm, and the storm was quiet. "Who is He?" the disciples whispered to each other. "Even the wind and the waves obey him!"

WAKE UP LITTLE GIRL

Luke 8:49-56

Jairus' daughter was very sick. He went to find Jesus and asked Him to come heal her. As they walked to Jairus' house, many other people wanted to talk to Jesus too. Jesus didn't hurry, but took time for everyone.

A servant came with bad
news. "It's too late for Jesus
to do anything. She is already
dead," he said.

But Jesus replied, "Don't
worry, just believe."

Jesus went to where the girl lay,
took her hand and said, "Little
girl, wake up!" The girl woke
up immediately, alive and well.
Everyone was amazed, and they
could not stop talking about what
they had just seen.

I LOVE KIDS

Matthew 14:18-19

One day a lot of parents brought
their children to meet Jesus. "The
Master is very busy, can't you
see?" the disciples told the parents.
They tried to shoo off the children
because they thought that Jesus did
not have time for them.

127

But Jesus disagreed. "No!" He said. "These children have a special place in My heart and in My kingdom!" Don't stand in their way, for every single child belongs to God."

HELP THE PEOPLE YOU MEET

Luke 10:25-37

Jesus once told a story:

A man was attacked by robbers. He lay helpless on the roadside, hurt and alone. Along came a man who worked in the temple, but he did not stop to help the man that was hurt. "It must be someone else's job to help him," he thought.

131

Then along came a Samaritan. He stopped and knelt down to bandage the wounds of the man who was hurt. Then he brought him to an inn. The Samaritan made sure that the man had food to eat so he could get well again.

"If you see someone in need of help," said Jesus, "go and help them! Don't think about who they are. Everyone is important to God. When you are kind to others, it pleases God."

WE ARE ALL IMPORTANT

Matthew 18:12-14

"Your Father in heaven greatly cares for everyone," Jesus told His friends one day. Then he told them this story:

A shepherd owned a hundred sheep. One day when he counted his sheep there were only ninety-nine in the fold. One sheep was missing!

The shepherd then left the ninety-nine
other sheep and went looking for the
one that was lost. He wouldn't stop
until he found it.

When he finally found it, he put the sheep

on his shoulders and carried it home. At

home he celebrated with his friends. This

is what God does too—He doesn't want

anyone to be lost.

ZACCHAEUS' DINNER WITH JESUS

Luke 19:1-19

Zacchaeus was a greedy man. He cheated people out of their money, so Zacchaeus didn't have many friends. One day Jesus came to town, but because Zacchaeus was very short, he couldn't see Jesus over the crowd.

Then Zaccheus decided to climb a tree to get a better view. When Jesus came to that tree, He stopped and looked up at Zaccheus. "Can I come eat at your house today?" Jesus asked Zaccheus.

Zacchaeus was so happy! "You are very welcome!" he said, jumping down from the tree. During the meal Zacchaeus stood up and said, "I will repay everybody that I have ever cheated!"

"This is exactly what a child of God should do!" Jesus told Zacchaeus.

BLESSED IS THE KING

Mark 11:8-10

When Jesus rode into Jerusalem,
everybody celebrated Him like He was
a mighty king. They danced and sang,
"Hosanna! Blessed is the King. He is
coming in the name of our God!"

People cheered Him on by waving with
palm leaves and placing their cloaks on
the street before Him. The people wanted
Jesus to fight against their enemies,
but Jesus wasn't a warrior king. Jesus
wanted to be king in their hearts.

REMEMBER JESUS

Luke 22:7–20

Jesus was sad because He knew He would soon die. He had a last meal with His disciples and said, "When I'm gone, remember me every time you eat together like we do now."

GETHSEMANE GARDEN

Matthew 26:36-39

After the meal, Jesus took his disciples to Gethsemane garden to pray. He was afraid and sad, so He prayed to God, "Father help me! Let Your will and not My will be done."

When Jesus had finished praying,

soldiers came to arrest Him. The soldiers

were sent by the leaders of the country.

They hated Jesus and said He was guilty

of serious crimes.

JESUS LOVES ME

John 3:16

The soldiers crucified Jesus. The disciples
and Jesus' friends were so sad. They
didn't understand that it was God's plan
for Jesus to die, in order to pay for all
the wrong things we have done.

By dying on the cross and coming back to life again, Jesus made sure that everyone who believes in Him will live with Him in Heaven forever—no matter who they are.

JESUS IS NOT DEAD

Matthew 28: 1-10

Jesus didn't stay dead! Three days later, two of Jesus' friends hurried out to His tomb. The big stone had been rolled aside, and an angel was sitting on it!

"Do not be afraid," the angel said. "Come and see: Jesus is not in the tomb anymore; He lives! Now hurry—go tell the disciples that He is alive!"

The women hurried on their way back
to town. Suddenly Jesus stood in front
of them. "Hello!" He said. "Don't be
afraid! Go and tell my friends that I
will meet them soon!"

JESUS IS ALWAYS WITH YOU

Matthew 28:18-20

Jesus met with His friends many times.
Right before He went back to be with His
Father in heaven, He said, "Remember this!
I am with you always. Even until the end
of the world!"

JESUS IS GOD'S SON

Matthew 16:15-16; Acts 2:21

Peter was one of Jesus' disciples. He told everyone he met about Jesus. "He is the son of the Living God," he said. "Anyone who believes in Him will be saved. Jesus wants every single person to know the love of the Father." Peter and the other disciples kept telling people about Jesus, and everyone who believed became part of God's family.